W9-AMN-023

Gardens

Animals in the
Garden

by Mari Schuh

Consulting Editor: Gail Saunders-Smith, PhD

Content Consultant: Sarah Pounders
Education Specialist, National Gardening Association

CAPSTONE PRESS
a capstone imprint

Pebble Books are published by Capstone Press,
151 Good Counsel Drive, P.O. Box 669, Mankato, Minnesota 56002.
www.capstonepress.com

Printed in the United States of America in North Mankato, Minnesota
092009
005618CGS10

Books published by Capstone Press are manufactured with paper
containing at least 10 percent post-consumer waste.

Library of Congress Cataloging-in-Publication Data
Schuh, Mari C., 1975–
    Animals in the garden / by Mari Schuh.
    p. cm. — (Pebble books. Gardens)
    Summary: "Simple text and photographs present animals found
in gardens" — Provided by publisher.
    Includes bibliographical references and index.
    ISBN 978-1-4296-3982-8 (library binding)
    ISBN 978-1-4296-4839-4 (paperback)
    1. Garden animals — Juvenile literature. I. Title. II. Series: Pebble
(Mankato, Minn). Gardens.
QL119.S38 2010
591.75′54 — dc22   2009025590

Note to Parents and Teachers

The Gardens set supports national science standards related to
life science. This book describes and illustrates animals found in
gardens. The images support early readers in understanding the
text. The repetition of words and phrases helps early readers
learn new words. This book also introduces early readers to
subject-specific vocabulary words, which are defined in the
Glossary section. Early readers may need assistance to read some
words and to use the Table of Contents, Glossary, Read More,
Internet Sites, and Index sections of the book.

Table of Contents

Full of Life

Gardens are full of life.
Some creatures are helpful,
but some are pests.

Garden Pests

Some creatures eat
garden plants.
Rabbits look for
lettuce and carrots
to nibble.

Curious raccoons
paw and snoop
through gardens.
Berries and tomatoes
are foods they like to eat.

Deer munch on corn
and apples.
Birds search for berries.

Helpful Creatures

Many animals
help gardens grow.
Ladybugs eat aphids
that hurt plants.

14

Spiders eat insects that eat plants.

Worms wiggle
through the soil.
Their droppings
add nutrients
that help plants grow.

18

Bees carry pollen
from flower to flower.
Flowers need pollen
to make new seeds.

At Home in the Garden

Gardens are home
to all sorts of animals.
How many animals
do you see?

Glossary

aphid — a tiny insect that sucks liquid from plants

creature — a living being such as an animal or person

insect — a small animal with a hard outer shell, six legs, three body sections, and two antennae; most insects have wings.

nutrient — something needed by plants to stay strong and healthy

pest — an animal that hurts, destroys, or eats flowers, fruit, vegetables, and other plant parts

pollen — tiny, yellow grains found in flowers

soil — the top layer of earth where plants can grow

Read More

Hewitt, Sally. *Local Wildlife: What's in My Garden?* Science Starters. North Mankato, Minn.: Stargazer Books, 2006.

Lambilly-Bresson, Elisabeth de. *Animals in the Garden.* Animal Show and Tell. Milwaukee: Gareth Stevens, 2007.

Woodward, John. *What Lives in the Garden?* What Lives in...? Milwaukee: Gareth Stevens, 2007.

Internet Sites

FactHound offers a safe, fun way to find Internet sites related to this book. All of the sites on FactHound have been researched by our staff.

Here's all you do:

Visit *www.facthound.com*

FactHound will fetch the best sites for you!

Index

Word Count: 110
Grade: 1
Early-Intervention Level: 14

Editorial Credits
Jenny Marks, editor; Heidi Thompson, designer; Marcie Spence, media
    researcher; Eric Manske, production specialist; Sarah Schuette,
    photo stylist; Marcy Morin, scheduler